THE SILENT DESTRUCTION

WRITTEN AND ILLUSTRATED BY
YASMIN S. BROWN

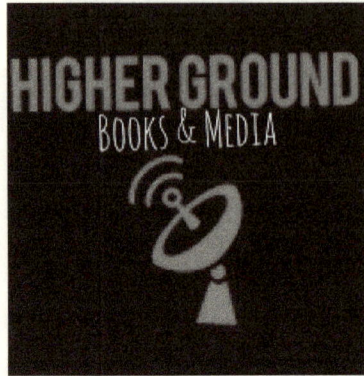

Higher Ground Books & Media
Springfield, Ohio.
http://highergroundbooksandmedia.com

Printed in the United States of America 2019

THE SILENT DESTRUCTION

TABLE OF CONTENTS

THE SILENT DESTRUCTION

Dedication

To all young girls and women that have kept silent. Know that you are beautiful inside and out. Self-destructive behavior doesn't have to be your only way out.

You have a voice inside of you waiting to fight back just know you are worth so much more.

THE SILENT DESTRUCTION

Introduction

Taquayasia was a beautiful young girl that enjoyed going to church and Sunday school. She also loved to hang out with her grandmother, great aunts, and great uncles. She would sit and talk to them for hours instead of hanging with her friends. Unknowingly one day her innocence would be taken away.

Innocence was taken away by molestation, suicide, date rape and abuse.

THE SILENT DESTRUCTION

THE SILENT DESTRUCTION

MOLESTATION

THE SILENT DESTRUCTION

One night while her mom was out enjoying her adult life Taquayasia's sister Shonnese had her friend Theresa stay over, which wasn't out of the ordinary since she visited over all the time. This night, however, while everyone was asleep, Theresa awakened Taquayasia with a gentle touch. Taquayasia did not understand what was going on. Theresa took Taquayasia's hands and placed them on her breast; then she kissed her. Taquayasia did not know what to do. In the morning, when she woke, Taquayasia kept quiet about what happened. She thought her sister might get angry at her, or worse, Shonnese might not believe her if she told. From that night on, every time Theresa stayed over, she repeated the same behavior. To try to avoid her, Taquayasia would stay with her cousin until one-night Larry -her cousin's brother - was home. When night fell, and everyone was fast asleep Larry came downstairs and got on top of Taquayasia while her cousin was sleeping right beside her. Larry started grinding on Taquayasia then kissing her while his penis was erect. Scared, Taquayasia bumped her cousin to wake up, and the brother ran back upstairs. Unsure of what she should do Taquayasia kept quiet so no one would get in trouble. After that night when her cousin would ask her to spend the night, she would decline. Not knowing what to do at this point since she doesn't want to stay home or with her cousin, she decides to start hanging with her friends more for a place to stay. A few months had gone by, and Shonnese's friend Theresa stopped visiting over. Taquayasia now felt safe to stay at home. To her

THE SILENT DESTRUCTION

surprise, the safety and peace that she felt would quickly fade away. The weekend was fast approaching, the sun was shining, and all was well until Shonnese walked into the house and uttered those words, "can Theresa spend the night?" Taquayasia's heart was racing as she awaited her mother's response. "Yes," her mother replied, as Taquayasia's thoughts raced. She went into panic mode, not knowing where she would stay that night. Saddened by the news, Taquayasia searched desperately for a friend's house where she might spend the night. She found a friend that she had been close to for a long time.

What Taquayasia didn't know was that her experience would be worse than if she had stayed the night with her cousin. She and her friend Holly played outside having a great time until the street lights came on and it was time to go in. Once Holly and Taquayasia went into the house they got their snacks and sat down to watch movies. They fell asleep as the film concluded. In the middle of the night, Holly's adult brother started touching Taquayasia. He climbed on top of her and started grinding then placed his fingers inside Taquayasia's vagina. Upset, scared, and confused Taquayasia leaves her friend's house in the middle of the night and goes home. Not knowing who to tell about what just happen she remains quiet. Taquayasia never told on anyone that he touched her inappropriately because she didn't want to get in trouble or get anyone else in trouble. Holding everything in that has happened to her, Taquayasia starts to act out.

THE SILENT DESTRUCTION

THE SILENT DESTRUCTION

Let's Talk

What should Taquayasia have done?

_____

_____

_____

_____

_____

_____

_____

_____

_____

_____

Should Taquayasia have told someone?

_____

_____

_____

_____

_____

_____

_____

_____

_____

_____

THE SILENT DESTRUCTION

Statistic Resource

- "Child Sexual Abuse - Facts for Families - aacap.org.
  http://www.aacap.org/AACAP/Families_and_yo uth/Facts_for_Families/FFF-Guide/Child-Sexual-Abuse-009.aspx

Attempted Suicide

THE SILENT DESTRUCTION

With everything that has happened to Taquayasia she began to get depressed. As she thought of all the bad things that had happened to her, she started to cry out for attention.   One day as her mother sat in the kitchen with her friends Taquayasia reached out to her, but she was too busy entertaining to notice. Seeking her mother's attention, Taquayasia decided to stick a metal majorette baton down her throat without the rubber tip finding her mother's care. Her mother got scared and angry all at the same time. Taquayasia never went to the doctor to see if she damaged anything and it was never mentioned again by her mother. Now Taquayasia felt even worse than she did before; she tried to pretend to feel better and look happy. Days had gone by and Taquayasia had been able to suppress her feelings of depression until one day the girls at school started saying mean things about her. The girls at school would call her sluts, whores and say she was weird. This hurt Taquayasia's already broken feelings. She started to feel sad all over. Once again Taquayasia kept everything bottled up inside and didn't tell anyone. One day while her mother was watching television in the living room, Taquayasia went into the kitchen and got a steak knife. Taquayasia snuck the knife into her room where she proceeded to cut her leg until she thought she felt better. Taquayasia walks out of her room as nothing happen placing the blade back in the kitchen, then going back into the living room. Hiding the cuts under her pants as she sat with her mother watching television. As night fell Taquayasia began feeling even more sad and confused about her

THE SILENT DESTRUCTION

life, as Shonnese walked into the house with Theresa. Things have now deteriorated for Taquayasia. Theresa came into Taquayasia's room as everyone was fast asleep in their place. The next morning Taquayasia felt worse than she did the night before. Not feeling up to going to school, Taquayasia asked her mother. Her mother told her "no" and she must go to school. Feeling even worse Taquayasia went into the bathroom open the medicine cabinet and proceeded to take all her mother's medication. Taquayasia became ill to the point of vomiting repeatedly. Her mother allowed her to stay home, but never spoke to her about her actions; of what had just happened. At this point Taquayasia was feeling unloved and started looking for love in all the wrong people.

THE SILENT DESTRUCTION

Let's Talk

What should Taquayasia's mother have done?

_____

_____

_____

_____

_____

_____

_____

_____

_____

_____

Do you think Taquayasia's mother should have talk to
her to try to find out the problem?

_____

_____

_____

_____

_____

_____

_____

_____

_____

_____

THE SILENT DESTRUCTION

Statistic Resource

- *if The Parent Resource Program The Jason Foundation, Youth Suicide Statics, 2018, prp.jasonfoundation.com/facts/youth-suicide-statistics/*

THE SILENT DESTRUCTION

DATE RAPE

THE SILENT DESTRUCTION

*O*n the search to find love on a beautiful summer evening Taquayasia was home alone while her mother and sister were out. Out of boredom Taquayasia decides to invite her friend Darion over to watch movies. Taquayasia always thought Darion was a sweet boy and she had a crush on him. When her friend arrived, he had a bottle of wine with him. Taquayasia had never drank before but since it was her friend she thought should try it. They popped in the movie Friday and Taquayasia got the popcorn. Her friend poured two glasses of wine. After she had two glasses of wine Taquayasia was feeling a little tipsy; not even noticing her friend didn't drink much of his wine. Darion liens in to kiss her during the movie and she reciprocates. They stop kissing and continue to watch some more of the film. Her friend then suggests they should go upstairs and talk. Feeling a little tipsy Taquayasia didn't think anything of it since they had hung out in her room before. During their conversation, he goes in for another kiss, she obliged. They stopped kissing and continued their discussion, but this time it got a little weird as Darion starts talking about all the different women he had been with intimately. Taquayasia finds that a little strange, but Darion thinks it's okay and goes in for another kiss. This time Taquayasia tells him to stop, so Darion forces her down on the bed and kisses her. Taquayasia did not respond and pushed him away. He grabs her and pushes her back down on the bed. She tells him no once again. He did not listen to her. His body now feels heavy on top of her. Taquayasia tries to get free, but he

THE SILENT DESTRUCTION

holds her wrist together with one hand. Taquayasia works to keep her legs together, but he put his knee between her legs. He used his other hand to remove Taquayasia's shorts. Once her shorts got pass the knee he then used his leg for the rest of the way. Darion then unbutton his pants and slid his erect penis between Taquayasia's legs pushing inside. Pent down with no place to go Taquayasia starts to cry. As his penis strokes increased her tears began to fall faster. Taquayasia is lying there lifeless while he is on top of her. After he finish he tells her he will never do it again because it did not feel the way he wanted it to feel; since there wasn't a response to him having sex with her. After he left Taquayasia cried some more then took a bath. Feeling ashamed and embarrassed Taquayasia was unsure on how to handle what just happen to her. Because Taquayasia thought it was her fault for inviting him over to hang out she never told anyone. A few months went by and Taquayasia confronted him about what happen. He called her a bitch, and tells her that she is lying. Darion said he didn't rape her and if he did he is sorry. She convinced herself it didn't happen and blocked it out of her mind. Trying to go on with her life was hard and she needed a way to release all the sadness and frustration that had built up inside her.

THE SILENT DESTRUCTION

Let's Talk

Should Taquayasia have called the police or told someone that can help her?

_____
_____
_____
_____
_____
_____
_____
_____
_____
_____

Was Taquayasia right by confronting Darion for raping her?

_____
_____
_____
_____
_____
_____
_____
_____
_____

THE SILENT DESTRUCTION

Statistic Resource

- Sexual Violence Against Youth & Young People | National https://www.nsvrc.org/projects/lifespan/sexual-violence-against-youth-young-people993)

Drugs/Promiscuity

THE SILENT DESTRUCTION

*F*eeling depressed Taquayasia starts looking for ways to release. She is longing for a sense of belonging, so she starts hanging out with a new set of friends. This new crew was bad news for her, but she never noticed. Blinded by all the pain and frustration she was holding inside Taquayasia never noticed what she was getting herself into. Taquayasia's new crew invites her to come hang out with them. Not knowing they like to turn up on a regular basis she accepts the invite. One Friday night Taquayasia goes to hang with her new set of friends and they are drinking, smoking marijuana, and popping pills. Not sure what to think she just stands there and observe the activity. One of her crew members offer her a drink and she accepts to fit in. Before she knew it, she was throwing back Old English mixed with slow gin, Mad Dog 20/20, and lots of other alcohol. Taquayasia has put down so much liquor that she is no longer a functioning drunk. She is lying on the cold cement and is unable to get up. A group of guys helps her up and takes her home, since one of them lives nearby. When they arrived at Taquayasia's house her mother was not home, so the guys invited themselves in to her house. One of the guys carried Taquayasia to her bedroom. He lays her in the bed and lays down beside her. The strange boy is now filling on her breast. Taquayasia tells him to stop then blacks out and never knew what happen after she uttered those words. The next day with a rough hangover Taquayasia went on as nothing happen. Later in the afternoon one of the girls from the crew called her to come hang out again; once again Taquayasia accepts. She finally gets

THE SILENT DESTRUCTION

up out of bed and gets dressed to meet up with her friends around 8:00 p.m. As soon as she walks in her friend's house red cups are flowing and the smell of marijuana in the air. After a few drinks Taquayasia is feeling a little tipsy, but not as drunk as the night before. One of the other crew members came over to Taquayasia on the couch with what she thought was a cigarette. The member offered Taquayasia a hit of what she now realizes is a blunt. Hesitant Taquayasia does it anyway because she didn't want to seem lame. She is now high and drunk without caring about her actions Taquayasia's hormones kick in. Taquayasia is now outside having sex with her male friend Jamie on a bench in a tunnel around the corner from her friend's house. The thickness of Jamie's penis hurt her at first but as he gently moved in and out she became submissive with relaxation. Taquayasia didn't care if anyone was watching all she could think of is how good she was feeling now as if someone cared about her. When they finished she went home and took a bath then to bed. The next day Taquayasia went outside and can hear the whispers of her behavior from last night. She now puts on this tuff attitude as her friend comes up to her and tells her what everyone is saying. Taquayasia tells her friend she doesn't care and shrugs it off. This makes Taquayasia drink even more and turns to promiscuity. Taquayasia starts hanging out by herself. Spiraling into a deeper depression Taquayasia stops hanging with her crew. Continuing to drink and smoke marijuana she graduates from bottom shelf alcohol to top-shelf vodka straight. Taquayasia is now sneaking into bars with fake identification every

THE SILENT DESTRUCTION

Thursday, Friday, and Saturday; sometimes Sunday. She starts to notice the more she drinks the more enraged her hormones become. Now she is having sex with different guys every weekend going to motels and even in her house when her mother wasn't home. Out of all the guys she was sexing she became really cool with one them name Aaron. Aaron and Taquayasia hung out a lot and things started to change as they started to get serious.

THE SILENT DESTRUCTION

Let's Talk

Do you think Taquayasia needs help?

_____
_____
_____
_____
_____
_____
_____
_____
_____
_____

Do you think Taquayasia is acting out from what has happened to her, experiencing peer pressure or both?

_____
_____
_____
_____
_____
_____
_____
_____
_____
_____

THE SILENT DESTRUCTION

Static Resource

- McNeill, Maggie, *"The Washington Post,"* *Lies, damned lies and sex work statistics, 2014,* *www.washingtonpost.com/news/the-watch/wp/2014/03/27/lies-damned-lies-and-sex-work-statistics/?utm_term=.b11479dcd48a*

THE SILENT DESTRUCTION

ABUSE

THE SILENT DESTRUCTION

*T*aquayasia has now slowed down on her drinking and going out to party since Aaron came into the picture. She genuinely fell for Aaron; he is nice and treats her like the world. Taquayasia decided that she should change for the better to keep him. Despite everything that has happen to her; she is able to put that aside and learn how to love. Little did Taquayasia know she was changing for the better but things were going to change for the worst. After dating Aaron for a year, this person, she thought was a gentleman turn into a possessive and angry person. After their first disagreement things became different in the relationship. One early afternoon after speaking with Aaron on the telephone Taquayasia went to visit him at his house. As she got closer to the door she noticed it was open. Taquayasia took a few more steps and seen two people on the couch a male and female, but she couldn't tell who was sitting there since he has brothers. As she drew nearer she notice the female was sitting on the male's lap. When Taquayasia got close to the door she noticed it was Aaron with no shirt; the girl with her pants and bra. The girl turned toward the door and Taquayasia noticed it was her cousin Marion. Upset Taquayasia walks in the door and her cousin jumps up then runs out the house. Aaron and Taquayasia began to argue about his actions. As the argument heated up Aaron strikes Taquayasia in the face. She holds her face and starts to cry. Aaron walks over to her then apologize saying he will never do it again; Taquayasia accepts his apology. Days had gone by and all is well with their relationship. They are now a happy couple

THE SILENT DESTRUCTION

again; so Taquayasia thought. The next day after having sex with her boyfriend she starts itching bad in her pubic hairs. She goes in to the bathroom to see why she is scratching so much and noticed her boyfriend had given her crabs. She once again confronts her boyfriend to tell him what she had found. Her boyfriend tells her he let his friend's sister where his pants and when she gave them back he didn't wash them before he wore them; that is how he got crabs. Now they began to argue about his cheating ways. As the argument rolls into the hallway of his house he pushes Taquayasia down the stairs. Taquayasia catches herself and only gets minor injuries, but this time she leaves the house and goes home. Aaron waits until Taquayasia cools down and calls her the next day. He once again apologizes and brings gifts to her house. Taquayasia wasn't sure if she should forgive him or tell someone, but she ends up forgiving him. Forgiving him, thinking things would get better they were back together. One nice sunny day Taquayasia's friend Shannon came over and they were gossiping about different things; Taquayasia has missed. Shannon tells Taquayasia, Aaron is cheating with her neighbor that lives in an upstairs apartment. Hurt, Taquayasia and her friend continued to talk then there was a knock at the door Shannon answers and it was Aaron. Aaron came in the door. Taquayasia asked him about her neighbor and he instantly became defensive. Taquayasia tells Aaron she wants to break up because of everything that had happened between them. He immediately becomes angry and headbutts Taquayasia in front of her friend. Shannon runs out the house to go get Taquayasia's

THE SILENT DESTRUCTION

mother from a nearby beer pub. When Shannon and Taquayasia's mother return Aaron was gone. Taquayasia is sitting in the living room crying with a knot on her head. Taquayasia's mother explained the importance about getting out of an unhealthy relationship and she never went back to Aaron.

THE SILENT DESTRUCTION

Let's Talk

Should Taquayasia have left Aaron or told her
mother/friend after the first time he hit her?

_____

_____

_____

_____

_____

_____

_____

_____

_____

_____

Do you think Aaron's apologies were sincere?

_____

_____

_____

_____

_____

_____

_____

_____

_____

_____

THE SILENT DESTRUCTION

Statistic Resource

- Fifth & Pacific Companies, Inc. (Liz Claiborne, Inc.), Conducted by Teen Research Unlimited, (May 2009). "Troubled Economy and Teen Dating Abuse | Break the Cycle. https://www.breakthecycle.org/dating-violence-research/troubled-economy-and-teen-dating-abuse" Available at breakthecycle.org/surveys

- Dating Abuse Statistics - Campus Safety. https://www.campussafetymagazine.com/safety/dating-abuse-statistics/highest rate of intimate partner violence — almost triple the national average.

Help

1. National Sexual Assault Hotline
   1-800-656-4673

2. National Suicide Prevention Lifeline
   1-800-273-8255

3. National Child Abuse Hotline
   1-800-422-4453

4. Teen Dating Abuse Hotline
   1-866-331-9474

5. Hope (Date Rape)
   1-800-656-4673

6. Rehab
   1-877-959-4116

7. Teen/Domestic Violence
   1-800-799-7233

THE SILENT DESTRUCTION

Never be afraid of your story, because it always becomes a victory in God's kingdom. Be strong in your testimony and watch God allow you to soar.

THE SILENT DESTRUCTION

Seeking help from a Mental Health Professional means you are no longer a victim but a victor in your personal victory.

Other titles from
Higher Ground Books & Media

Wise Up to Rise Up by Rebecca Benston

A Path to Shalom by Steen Burke

From a Hole in My Life to a Life Made Whole by

Janet Kay Teresa

Overcomer by Forrest Henslee

Miracles: I Love Them by Forest Godin

32 Days with Christ's Passion by Mark Etter

The Magic Egg by Linda Phillipson

The Tin Can Gang by Chuck David

Whobert the Owl by Mya C. Benston

Add these titles to your collection today!

HigherGroundBooksandMedia.com

THE SILENT DESTRUCTION

www.ingramcontent.com/pod-product-compliance
Lightning Source LLC
Chambersburg PA
CBHW021922040426
42448CB00007B/864